What did I do on my summer vacation?

I went on a Recycle Road Trip! Picking up trash wherever I would stop, out I would pop to see what things, if any, were just lying on the ground, stuck in a bush or blown into a tree.

It's amazing all the different items that I found, some new, some old, but, no matter what, there was always something. Most everything I collected could be reused and most certainly everything I found could be recycled or composted.

Do elephant seals in San Simeon eat cigarette butts?
Do ravens in Richmond need an expired phone card?
Do coyotes in the Coachella Valley need cups?

The answer to all those questions is of course, no! Do we want to be contributing to creating that kind of environment? Is it good for us? Again, no!

So by sifting through sand, soil and sea, I have found a variety of ordinary and interesting objects in places where they have no business being. So join me on this inventive and eco-friendly expedition. On my treasure trash map, I will show you where materials have ended up. I will also show you how we can change; how we can make sure trash doesn't travel far and wide.

Table of Contents

Trashy But True

According to the *United States Environmental Protection Agency,* in 2007, Americans generated 245 million tons of trash and of that trash, recycled and/or composted 85 million tons.

- On average, 4.6 pounds per person is generated every day and 1.5 pounds of that figure is recycled.

- If just 25% of families in the United States used ten fewer plastic bags per month, we would save over 2.5 million bags per year.

- Every year we throw away 24,000,000 tons of leaves and grass.

- Every ton of recycled office paper saves 280 gallons of water.

- Research, according to *Keep California Beautiful*, indicates that litter comes from seven primary sources:
     pedestrians
     drivers
     household garbage cans
     commercial dumpsters
     construction sites
     loading docks
     uncovered trucks

Remarkable Recycling

In addition to what the average American is generating and trying to recycle, there are all sorts of incredible recycling innovations going on around the country.

- **Raising the roof!** In Michigan, *Crutchall Resource Recycling* tears off roof shingles and converts them into road material. Roof shingles are made from asphalt and aggregate which are the same ingredients used to make roads. It is estimated that Michigan generates nearly one million tons of tear-off shingles every year.

- **Hair it is!** At *Matter of Trust* in San Francisco, California, yes, they recycle hair by working with salons throughout the United States to collect hair clippings to soak up oil spills.

- **Just a flush away!** At *Enviroglas* in Plano, Texas, porcelain toilets are recycled into floors and counter tops.

- **Red light, green light!** The colored glass from retired street signals in Chicago, Illinois is recycled into glass rocks and used as ground cover for landscaping projects.

- **Roll tape.** At *Alternative Community Training* (ACT), individuals with disabilities recycle donated video cassettes and floppy disks by erasing the contents, repackaging and selling them for reuse.

Our Cup Runneth Over

In 2010, it is estimated that 16 billion paper cups will be used for serving coffee. That amount is the equivalent of more than 6.5 million trees being cut down, 4 billion gallons of water used and ample energy utilized to power 54,000 homes for a year.

You can recycle the cup and reuse the cardboard coffee sleeve to create this Recycle Masquerade, a recycled version of the colorful and dramatic masks that originated in Venice, Italy in the 13th Century.

SCRAPS AND STUFF NEEDED:

Cardboard coffee sleeve

Stick or dowel

Assortment of ribbons, caps, buttons, stickers, feathers, etc.

White glue

Scissors

DIRECTIONS

1. Draw out two eyes on sleeve and cut out.
2. Punch two holes on one side of sleeve and slide dowel through to make the mask handle.
3. Decorate and glue assorted materials on front of mask.
4. Let dry and masquerade!

Recycle Bugs

No litter bugs in this project!

Far from being a litter bug, you can make this insect by reusing scraps and strips. When your bug has "outlived" its shelf-life, you can recycle all the parts!

SCRAPS AND STUFF NEEDED:

Plastic four-pack holder

Yarn

Fabric scraps

Bug eyes or buttons

Sequins

Pipe cleaner

Stickers

DIRECTIONS

1. Bend pipe cleaner in a half and twist around one end of skeleton (plastic form). You have now made the antennae.

2. Wrap furry, nubby and colorful yarn around rest of plastic, creating the body.

3. Decorate body with sequins, fabric scraps (can be used to make wings) or anything bug-like, if desired.

4. Glue eyes on the plastic at the antennae end.

5. You have now designed your very own Recycle Bug!

Put A Cork On It!

Cork is not only reusable;
it is recyclable.

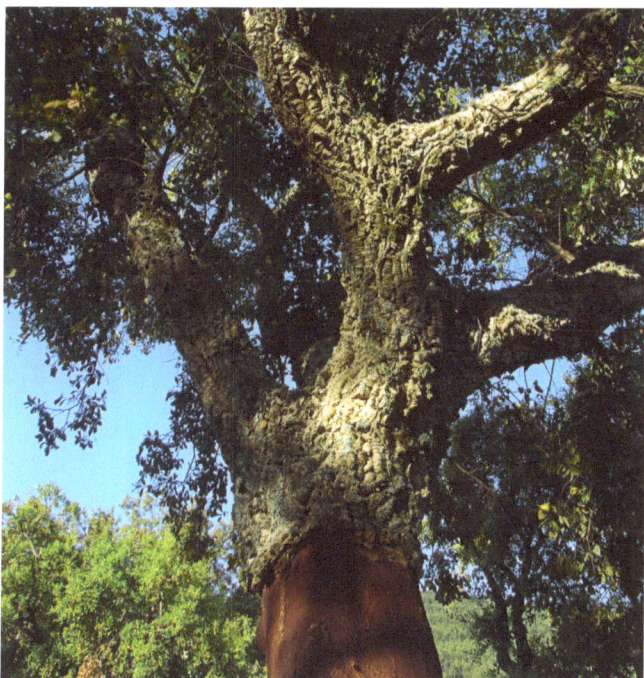

Cork is a natural product that comes from the Cork Oak tree. Cork forests are located primarily in the Mediterranean. The forests help drain millions of tons of carbon dioxide from the atmosphere. Carbon dioxide is a greenhouse gas. Increased emissions of greenhouse gases cause an increase in the Earth's surface temperature resulting in global climate change which effect the environment. According to the *National Aeronautics and Space Administration* (NASA) occurrences of climate change include shrinking glaciers, plant and animal ranges shifting and trees flowering sooner.

SCRAPS AND STUFF NEEDED:

Corks and/or cork board tiles (if making bulletin board)

Old frames

Photos

DIRECTIONS:

1. Arrange cork design prior to gluing.
2. Glue corks directly to the frame.
3. To add more dimension, stack corks on first cork layer.
4. When corks glued to frame have dried completely, insert favorite photo. For bulletin board, glue cork tile to the back of frame.

It's A Wonderful World

What's your view of the world?

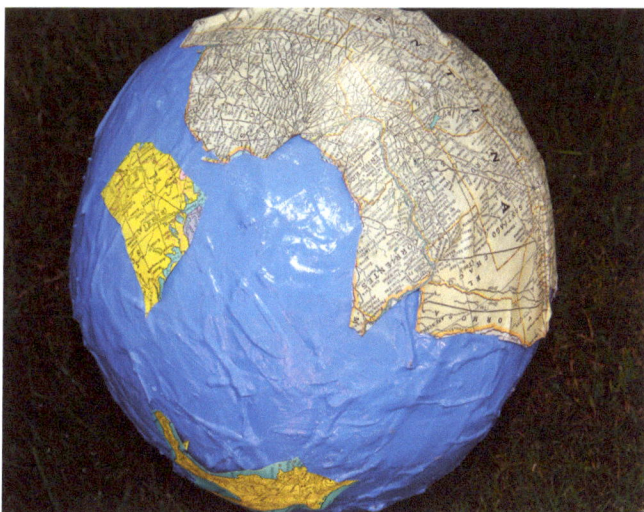

Create your own world easily with this paper mache project.

SCRAPS AND STUFF NEEDED:

Newspaper

Balloon

Acrylic gesso

Acrylic paints

Old maps

Paper mache paste

PASTE RECIPE:

¾ cup glue to ¼ cup water, stir together

DIRECTIONS:

1. Blow up a round balloon to desired size and tie off the end.

2. Tear newspaper into one-inch strips. Dip strips in glue mixture, skimming off excess, and apply to balloon. Leave at least a two-inch diameter at the bottom of the balloon.

3. Apply three layers of newspaper and let dry overnight.

4. Apply acrylic gesso to your globe and again let dry overnight. At this point, you can remove the balloon by popping it or by letting the air dissipate.

5. Paint the globe desired color or colors. Decoupage images from old maps using the same glue mixture.

Put Your Thinking Cap On!

Americans go through 2.5 million plastic bottles every hour. These bottles can be recycled, but what about the caps?

Plastic bottle caps jam recycling equipment and are generally not recycled at your local recycling center. The caps fall through the environmental crack, so to speak, and end up as litter on the side of the road, in our streams, in our rivers and most harmfully, in our oceans where they pose a danger to wildlife. In the waters, to birds and fish, they are mistaken for food. These plastic caps contain toxins that can be fatal to the animals and the environment which they live in and eventually the environment that we live in.

What should we do? Put our thinking caps on for the environment by collecting plastic bottle caps that we can recycle and reuse. Aveda, the beauty and haircare company, has a program that recycles caps.

SCRAPS AND STUFF NEEDED:

Plastic caps in a variety of colors from soda, margarine, detergent, milk, pet food and other plastic containers

Wood or cardboard for backing

Acrylic paint

Tab from aluminum can

DIRECTIONS:

1. Find sturdy cardboard or a scrap piece of wood for the background. Paint if desired.

2. Arrange design on board and start gluing.

3. Add dimension with color and cap layering.

4. When artwork is completely dried, glue aluminum tab on the back to hang the cap collage.

52 Pickup

Here is a list of trash picked up "on the road" during a three month period.

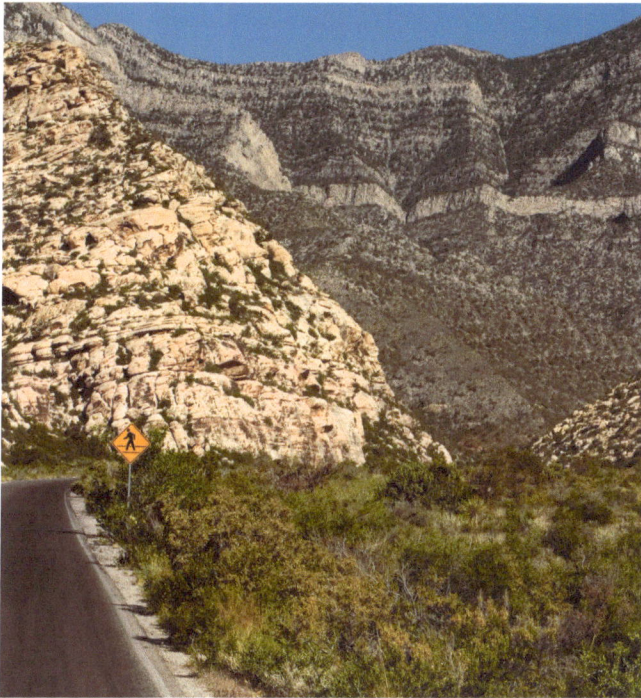

Batteries	Ice cream cups	Postcards
Beer cans	Junk mail	Potato chip bag
Broken glass	Keys	Receipts
Buttons	Magazines	Shampoo bottle
CDs	Milk carton	Shoe
Camera	Mylar	Soda pop bottle
Cards	Newspaper	Spatula
Cell phones	Paint	Spray cans
Chain	Pens	Styrofoam
Clips	Phone cards	Sunglasses
Coffee cups	Plastic bags	Sweatshirt
Coin purse	Plastic bleach bottle	Tags
Costume jewelry	Plastic comb	Ten dollar bill
Flag	Plastic silverware	Toys
Foam	Plastic soda bottles	Vinyl record
Hand lotion bottle	Political ads	Watches
Hub cap	Popsicle stick	Candy wrapper
	Take-out carton	

ECO GLOSSARY

Afforestation – the process of establishing a forest on land not previously forested

Biodegradable – material broken down into simple chemical compounds by bacterial, fungal and/or freely occurring biochemical actions

Carbon Footprint – is the measure of the impact human activities have on the environment in terms of the amount of greenhouse gases produced, measured in units of carbon dioxide

Climate Change – Increased emissions of greenhouse gases cause an increase in the Earth's surface temperature resulting in visible effects on the environment; the Intergovernmental *Panel of Climate Change* (IPCC) forecasts a temperature rise of 2.5 to 10 degrees Fahrenheit over the next century

Compost – the material resulting from natural breakdown of organic material by bacteria, fungi and other organisms; composted materials are used to enrich soil

Consumption – using of goods and services by a consumer

Disposable – item that is designed for a one-time use

Environment – all of the conditions, circumstances, processes and influences surrounding and affecting the development of an organism or group of organisms

Green – both in description and color, a word that has become a symbol for describing ecology and environmental awareness and responsibility

Landfill – large, outdoor zone used to dispose of garbage by burying it

Litter – trash that has been discarded without care or concern for its proper disposal

Municipal Solid Waste – solid waste produced by residential, commercial and institutional entities; does not include hazardous or agricultural wastes

Nonrecyclable – products that cannot be reprocessed or remanufactured

Recycle – to turn something old into something new; separating a material from waste and processing it again into another form

Reduce – to lessen the amount generated

Reuse – to use again

Resource – Something that is found in nature and is useful:
   1. Renewable Resource is a resource that can be replaced.
   2. Nonrenewable Resource is a resource that cannot be replaced.

Responsibility – able to make moral or rational decisions and therefore answerable for one's behavior; based on or showing good judgment

Source Reduction – reducing the generation of waste at the source through proper planning and management

Stewardship – the careful and responsible management of something entrusted to one's care; protection of the environment for the future benefit of generations of human beings by developing relevant institutions and strategies

Sustainability – the ability to support, endure or keep economically without depleting or damaging resources; providing for today, preserving for tomorrow

Trash – any material considered nonrecyclable; also referred to as "garbage"

Waste – anything that is no longer of use; unwanted or discarded

Associação Portuguesa de Cortiça
  www.realcork.org
Earth 911
  www.earth911.org
International Paper
  www.internationalpaper.com
Kansas Green School Network
  www.kansasgreenschools.org
Massachusetts Department of Environmental Protection
  www.mass.gov/dep

More Information & Sources

Matter of Trust
  www.matteroftrust.org
Michigan Department of Energy, Labor & Economic Growth
  www.michigan.gov/deqrecycling
National Aeronautics and Space Administration
  http://climate.nasa.gov/effects/
Recycle Caps with Aveda
  www.aveda.com
S.C.R.A.P. Gallery – The Art Museum for the Environment
  www.scrapgallery.org
United States Environmental Protection Agency
  www.epa.gov

ABOUT THE AUTHOR

Karen Riley is the Executive Director and a founder of the S.C.R.A.P. Gallery (Student Creative Recycle Art Program), the environmental arts education program for students within the Coachella Valley in Riverside County, California. Since 1997, the S.C.R.A.P. Gallery has been addressing two of today's most urgent issues – the environment and the education of youth throughout the Coachella Valley and beyond.

S.C.R.A.P.'s mission is to actively engage youth as stewards of their environment through a concentrated, hands-on, educational effort stressing the FOUR R'S – REDUCE, REUSE, RECYCLE, RESPONSIBILITY. The S.C.R.A.P. Gallery provides a link between industry, education, the arts and the environment through its Field Trip Program featuring environmental presentations, exhibits and self-directed art workshops using recycled and reused materials diverted from the landfill.

Riley received her Bachelor's Degree in Journalism from California State University Long Beach and her Master's Degree in Environmental Education from Fairfax University. She is also the author of *Landfill Lunch Box, Argollas Plasticas y Otras Cosas/Plastic Rings and Other Things, Don't Trash My Planet* and *The Eco Deck.*